THE HEALED SOUL

DEVOTIONAL WORKBOOK

A Journey Toward Healing, Wholeness, and Freedom

BY ELLASIN D. ALLEN, MS, LPC

THE HEALED SOUL

Published by

iPress Publishing

Newport News, Virginia

www.ipresspublishing.com

Unless otherwise indicated, all Scripture quotations are taken from the **King James Version (KJV)** of the Holy Bible.

Printed in the United States of America

For more information or for bulk purchases, please visit

www.ipresspublishing.com

ISBN: 978-1-969504-07-5

Cover design by **iPress Publishing**

Interior design by **Tessy Ogidi**

CONTENTS

INTRODUCTION

The Healed Soul Devotional Workbook is a companion on your journey toward emotional, spiritual, and mental wholeness. Through reflection, prayer, and practical exercises, each chapter invites you to explore a deeper layer of healing. You will encounter Scriptures, therapeutic insights, and soul-searching questions designed to help you process pain, renew your mind, and rediscover your peace in God.

HOW TO USE THIS WORKBOOK

- ☑ Read each chapter carefully, allowing time for reflection and prayer.

- ☑ Write your thoughts honestly in the journaling spaces provided.

- ☑ Engage with the interactive activities to apply what you learn.

- ☑ Meditate on the devotional Scriptures and allow the Holy Spirit to speak to you.

- ☑ Revisit sections as often as needed. Healing is a process, not a destination.

CHAPTER

One

STAINED
AND
TAINTED

Chapter Overview

There are moments in life when the stains of our past feel permanent, when shame whispers that what was done to us or by us defines who we are. This chapter invites you to bring every blemish before the God who cleanses, not condemns. Through honesty and surrender, the stains that once marked you become the very evidence of His mercy and restoration.

Expanded Insight

In therapy, we often talk about core beliefs, those silent conclusions we make about ourselves after trauma or rejection. Spiritually, these beliefs become the enemy's canvas for distortion. But God paints truth over every lie.

You are not what happened to you. You are not the mistakes you made. Healing begins when you allow God to reveal the difference between what was done and who you are.

When shame is exposed to grace, it loses its power. When trauma meets truth, healing begins. Your story may include pain, but it is not your identity; it's the soil from which wholeness can grow.

CHAPTER ONE

REFLECTIVE *Questions*

✅ What experiences or memories still make you feel "stained," and why?

....

....

....

....

✅ How have you allowed shame to define your worth or relationships?

....

....

....

....

✅ What would it mean to truly believe that you are forgiven and free?

....

....

....

✓ Who might you need to forgive, including yourself, to step into healing?

....

....

....

....

✓ When has God already shown you mercy that you overlooked?

....

....

....

....

✓ How can you begin speaking words of cleansing and truth over your life daily?

....

....

....

....

INTERACTIVE *Activities* 

1. **The Mirror Declaration**

   Stand before a mirror and say aloud:

   "I am not what was done to me. I am who God says I am, whole, loved, and restored." Repeat this declaration for seven days. Each day, write one truth God reveals about you.

2. **Cleansing Script Exercise**

   On a sheet of paper, list the labels or lies you've believed ("unworthy," "dirty," "broken"). Then, beside each one, write a cleansing truth from God's Word ("washed," "chosen," "redeemed"). Tear the paper into pieces and whisper, "These no longer define me."

3. **Grace Letter**

   Write a letter to your younger self or to the version of you who carried the most shame. Use compassionate language. End with: "Grace found me here, and I am free."

Devotional

"Purge me with hyssop, and I shall be clean; Wash me, and I shall be whiter than snow. Make me hear joy and gladness, that the bones You have broken may rejoice. Create in me a clean heart, O God, and renew a steadfast spirit within me."

David's prayer was not only for forgiveness but for transformation. He knew that sin and sorrow stain the soul, yet he also knew that God could cleanse it more deeply than the offense itself. Healing is not pretending the stain never existed; it is allowing God to change the meaning of that stain.

Where shame once spoke of guilt, it now speaks of grace. Every scar becomes a testimony that mercy triumphed over judgment. You are already being made new every day that you choose transparency over hiding.

JOURNAL *Reflection*

✔ What is God purging from your heart in this season?

....

....

....

....

....

✔ What does "renewing a steadfast spirit" mean to you personally?

....

....

....

....

....

PRAYER OF *Healing* *and Encouragement*

Father,

Thank you for seeing me when I felt unseen. Thank you for washing the places that still carry residue from my past. Where shame whispered "unclean," You declared "forgiven."

Lord, create in me a clean heart and renew my spirit. Let Your grace run through every hidden corner of my soul until no stain remains. Teach me to receive Your mercy without guilt and to walk boldly in the freedom You've provided.

I surrender the memories, the words, and the wounds that made me doubt my worth. Today, I stand as one who is redeemed, restored, and made whole. My stains tell Your story of grace.

In Jesus' name, Amen.

PERSONAL *Reflection*

CHAPTER
Two

THE OUTSIDER IN THE FAMILY

Chapter Overview

Every family has its rhythm, and sometimes, that rhythm plays a song we never learned to dance to. When rejection, favoritism, or misunderstanding enters the home, a soul can start to believe it was born wrong, unwanted, or unseen. This chapter invites you to confront that wound: the ache of being "the other one." God never meant for you to live as an outsider. He gathers, adopts, and restores the ones who were cast aside.

Expanded Insight

As a therapist, I've seen how early experiences of exclusion shape identity. Children who grow up feeling invisible often carry those patterns into adulthood, people-pleasing, over-performing, or isolating to avoid rejection. Spiritually, this creates a false narrative: "If my family didn't see me, why would God?"

But the truth is, God has always been intentional about choosing the overlooked. David was the forgotten shepherd boy. Joseph was the betrayed brother. Jesus was born in a manger, not a mansion. Rejection in your earthly family does not disqualify you from divine belonging; it positions you for spiritual adoption.

Healing begins when you stop defining yourself by whoever walked away and start identifying with the One who took you in.

REFLECTIVE *Questions*

- ☑ When did you first feel like an outsider in your family or community?

  ....

  ....

  ....

  ....

- ☑ How did that feeling influence how you show up in relationships today?

  ....

  ....

  ....

  ....

- ☑ What messages about worth or acceptance did you internalize as a child?

  ....

  ....

  ....

CHAPTER TWO

☑ In what ways have you over-functioned (or withdrawn) to earn love?

....

....

....

....

☑ How does knowing God calls you chosen to reframe your family story?

....

....

....

....

☑ Who do you now need to extend grace to, not for their sake, but for your own freedom?

....

....

....

....

INTERACTIVE *Activities* 

1. **Belonging Timeline**

   Draw a line representing your life. Mark key moments when you felt excluded or unseen, and then add moments when God reminded you of your value. Look for the pattern of His pursuit. He has been rewriting your belongings all along.

2. **Family Letter of Release**

   Write a letter (you never have to send it) to the person or people who made you feel like an outsider. Express your pain, your feelings, and your decision to release their approval. End with: "I am no longer defined by your silence. I belong to God, who calls me His own."

3. **Scripture Mirror Affirmation**

   Stand before a mirror and declare aloud:

   "I am accepted in the Beloved. I am not an outsider in the Kingdom of God." Repeat this daily for seven days. After each declaration, journal one way God affirmed your worth that day.

Devotional

EPHESIANS 1:4–6 (NKJV)

"Just as He chose us in Him before the foundation of the world, that we should be holy and without blame before Him in love, having predestined us to adoption as sons and daughters by Jesus Christ to Himself, according to the good pleasure of His will, to the praise of the glory of His grace, by which He made us accepted in the Beloved."

God did not choose you out of pity; He chose you on purpose. Long before any parent spoke your name, your identity was written in His will. Rejection wounds the soul because it attacks the core need to belong, but adoption heals it by establishing belonging that cannot be revoked. You are not a substitute child in God's family; you are His delight. The arms that others folded are the same ones He opens wide to embrace you.

JOURNAL *Reflection*

✓ What does being "accepted in the Beloved" mean to you personally?

....

....

....

....

....

✓ How can you begin embracing spiritual belonging even if your earthly family never affirms you?

....

....

....

....

....

PRAYER OF *Healing and Encouragement*

Father,

Thank you for calling me your child, even when I felt forgotten. Thank You for receiving me when those I longed for turned away. Today, I release the need to be validated by people who could not see my worth. Heal the places where rejection took root; pull up every lie that says I am unworthy of love.

Lord, teach me to rest in Your acceptance. Remind me that I am chosen, adopted, and secured in Your family. Help me extend the same grace to others that You continually give to me.

I belong to You. I am seen, known, and loved.

In Jesus' name, Amen.

PERSONAL *Reflection*

CHAPTER
Three

BROKEN SCATTERED PIECES

Chapter Overview

There are seasons when life feels shattered beyond repair, when the pieces of who we once were lie scattered across our past. Broken trust, unmet expectations, betrayal, or trauma can make us wonder if wholeness is even possible.

But what if the breaking wasn't the end? What if it was the beginning of transformation? This chapter reminds us that brokenness in the hands of God becomes beauty. The fragments of your story are not wasted; they are waiting for divine reconstruction.

Expanded Insight

In psychology, we often discuss integration, the process of bringing fragmented parts of the self back into unity. Trauma divides the mind and heart; healing brings them back into harmony. Spiritually, God specializes in integration.

When we've been broken, we tend to hide the pieces that don't look "perfect." But God asks us to bring every part, especially the ones we'd rather throw away. He doesn't discard you because of your damage; He rebuilds you with purpose.

Think of Kintsugi, the Japanese art of repairing pottery with gold. The artist doesn't conceal the cracks; they highlight them. The fractures become the most beautiful part of the piece. In the same way, your healing will not erase your pain; it will reveal your redemption.

When your brokenness is surrendered, your story becomes a vessel for others' healing.

REFLECTIVE *Questions*

- What life event caused you to feel the most "broken," and how did it shape your beliefs about yourself or God?

....

....

....

....

- What pieces of your story are you still trying to hide or fix on your own?

....

....

....

....

- How might you invite God into those areas of your life instead of avoiding them?

....

....

....

CHAPTER THREE

✅ Who has been able to see beauty in your brokenness, and what did that teach you?

....

....

....

....

✅ What does it mean for you personally that God can use "all things" (Romans 8:28) for your good?

....

....

....

....

✅ What new story might emerge if you stop trying to be perfect and start being present?

....

....

....

....

INTERACTIVE *Activities* 

1. **Fragments of Grace Exercise**

    Write down the "pieces" of your life that feel shattered, relationships, regrets, or losses. Next to each one, write how God has sustained or taught you through it. Then pray: "God, make these pieces shine with Your glory."

2. **Visual Healing Collage**

    Gather old magazines or images and create a collage that represents your healing journey. Include words like hope, restoration, peace, and grace. Hang it somewhere visible as a reminder that beauty can come from brokenness.

3. **Kintsugi Declaration**

    On a piece of paper, draw cracks representing broken moments of your life. Trace them over with gold or yellow ink and label each line with what God has restored: faith, courage, identity, joy. Repeat aloud: "My cracks are where His glory shines through."

Devotional

2 CORINTHIANS 4:7–9 (NKJV)

"But we have this treasure in earthen vessels, that the excellence of the power may be of God and not of us. We are hard-pressed on every side yet not crushed; we are perplexed, but not in despair; persecuted but not forsaken; struck down, but not destroyed."

Paul reminds us that we carry divine treasure inside fragile vessels. The cracks in your vessel don't disqualify you; they reveal where His light escapes. Every pressure, every heartbreak, every season of despair has a purpose: it teaches you to rely on God's strength instead of your own.

Brokenness is not the end of your story. It is the sacred place where grace gathers the scattered pieces and turns them into a testimony of endurance and faith.

JOURNAL *Reflection*

✅ What "treasure" has God revealed through your broken moments?

....

....

....

....

....

✅ How can you allow your scars to become someone else's source of hope?

....

....

....

....

....

PRAYER OF *Healing and Encouragement*

Father,

I thank You that You are near to the brokenhearted. You never turn away from my pain; you meet me in it. Today, I give You every shattered piece of my heart, trusting You to make something beautiful from what was broken.

Lord, teach me to see my cracks as proof of Your mercy. When I feel scattered, Lord, remind me that You are the Potter and I am the clay. Hold me together when I feel undone and let Your Spirit fill every empty space within me.

Thank You for transforming my brokenness into beauty, my sorrow into strength, and my wounds into wisdom. You are the God who restores, and I am living proof of it.

In Jesus' name, Amen.

PERSONAL *Reflection*

CHAPTER
Four

HEALING DEMANDS HONESTY

Chapter Overview

Healing is not for the faint of heart. It requires truth, raw, uncomfortable, and often painful truth. We cannot heal from what we continue to hide. Honesty is the doorway through which freedom walks.

In this chapter, we confront the tendency to minimize, excuse, or spiritualize our pain instead of facing it. True healing begins where denial ends. God's grace is not intimidated by your truth; it's drawn to it.

You will learn that honesty doesn't make you weak; it makes you ready. Ready for growth, ready for peace, and ready for God to restore what you've buried.

Expanded Insight

In counseling, we often say, "You can't change what you won't confront." Avoidance may protect you in the short term, but it keeps you trapped in the long term. Emotional honesty is the key that unlocks spiritual and psychological restoration.

Many of us learned early on to suppress our emotions, to smile when we wanted to scream, to serve when we needed to speak. But suppression is not healing. God invites you to bring the whole truth before Him, not the edited version.

Even Jesus modeled this when He cried out in Gethsemane, "My soul is exceedingly sorrowful, even to death" (Matthew 26:38). If the Son of God could express the weight of His pain, then so can we.

Honesty before God is not rebellion; it's a relationship. When we confess our wounds, He doesn't condemn us; He begins to clean them.

REFLECTIVE *Questions*

✓ What emotions do you find most difficult to admit, even to yourself?

....

....

....

....

✓ How have you learned to mask or suppress your true feelings?

....

....

....

....

✓ When have you told yourself, "I'm fine," when you really weren't?

....

....

....

....

☑ What would emotional honesty look like in your relationship with God today?

....

....

....

....

☑ What fears arise when you think about telling your truth?

....

....

....

....

☑ How can being honest become an act of worship rather than weakness?

....

....

....

....

INTERACTIVE Activities 

1. Truth-Telling Journal

Take 10 minutes to write a journal entry beginning with, "If I'm being honest with myself…" Don't censor your words. Let everything flow. When you're done, ask the Holy Spirit to highlight one truth He wants to heal.

2. Emotional Mapping Exercise

Draw a heart on a blank page and write inside it the emotions you've been carrying: anger, sadness, shame, fear, guilt. Then draw arrows pointing outward from each word and write one healthy way you can begin to release it (prayer, therapy, boundaries, forgiveness).

3. Confession as Cleansing

Read 1 John 1:9 aloud. Write a short confession, not just of sin, but of pain. Say, "Lord, this hurt me… and I'm ready to heal." Tear the page in half as a physical act of release.

Devotional

PSALM 139:23–24 (NKJV)

"Search me, O God, and know my heart; Try me and know my anxieties; And see if there is any wicked way in me And lead me in the way everlasting."

David didn't just ask God to fix him; he asked God to search him. That is the posture of a soul ready for transformation. Healing demands that we stop hiding the truth about what we think, feel, and believe. When you allow God to reveal what's hidden, He doesn't do it to shame you but to set you free.

Honesty is sacred. It's where pretension dies and intimacy with God begins. Every tear you cry in truth becomes a seed of freedom that will bloom in time.

JOURNAL *Reflection*

- ✓ What truth is God asking you to face today?

....

....

....

....

....

- ✓ How does honesty draw you closer to Him?

....

....

....

....

....

PRAYER OF *Healing and Encouragement*

Father,

I come before You without filters or masks. You know my heart, my fears, my failures, and my pain. Teach me to stop hiding behind strength and to start healing through honesty.

Search me, Lord. Reveal the areas I've buried beneath shame or silence. Help me to tell myself the truth, even when it hurts, so that Your light can reach the deepest parts of me.

Thank you for loving me enough to confront me. I permit you to rearrange what's been broken and to restore what's been buried. Let truth be the foundation of my healing and honesty the evidence of my faith.

In Jesus' name, Amen.

PERSONAL *Reflection*

CHAPTER
Five

REDEEMED FROM THE FRAGMENTS

Chapter Overview

There comes a time in every healing journey when we realize that restoration is not about returning to who we were before the pain; it's about becoming who God always intended us to be. Redemption means that even the broken, scattered fragments of our past have value in the Master's hands.

This chapter reminds you that you are not defined by what broke you, but by who redeemed you. Every fragment of your story, the good, the painful, the hidden, can become a vessel for glory. God doesn't just heal wounds; He repurposes them.

Your life is not a pile of unusable pieces; it's a mosaic of mercy.

Expanded Insight

In therapy, we talk about integration, the process of gathering the separated, unacknowledged parts of yourself and bringing them back into wholeness. Spiritually, redemption is God's version of integration.

Where trauma once fragmented your sense of self, grace gathers you again. Every piece you thought was worthless becomes a part of your testimony.

The story of redemption doesn't erase the pain; it reframes it. You may still see the cracks, but now they're filled with the gold of His glory.

When Joseph told his brothers, "You meant evil against me, but God meant it for good" (Genesis 50:20), he was declaring a universal truth: the very thing that broke you is often the thing God uses to build you.

Wholeness is not perfection; it's restoration with evidence of grace.

REFLECTIVE *Questions*

- ✓ What areas of your life still feel fragmented or disconnected?

....

....

....

....

- ✓ How has God already begun redeeming parts of your story you once resented?

....

....

....

....

- ✓ What does it mean to you that "nothing is wasted" in God's plan?

....

....

....

☑ How can you begin viewing your scars as sacred instead of shameful?

45

....

....

....

....

☑ What lessons have your fragments taught you about strength, endurance, or faith?

....

....

....

....

☑ Who in your life could benefit from hearing the redeemed version of your story?

....

....

....

....

INTERACTIVE *Activities* 

1. **The Mosaic of Me Exercise**

    Draw or print out a heart shape. Inside, write different words or phrases that represent pieces of your story, both beautiful and broken. Around the heart, write these words in bold: Redeemed. Restored. Whole. Thank God aloud for every piece that made you who you are.

2. **"What the Enemy Meant for Evil" Journal**

    Write a short list of painful moments that once caused you to feel broken. Beside each, write how God has turned or is turning that moment for your good. Pray through Genesis 50:20, thanking God for His redemptive work in your life.

3. **Restoration Affirmations**

    Write or repeat these aloud:

    "God is redeeming my story."

    "My fragments are becoming my foundation."

    "Nothing in my life is wasted."

    Add your own affirmation that speaks directly to your healing journey.

Devotional

ISAIAH 61:3–4 (NKJV)

"To console those who mourn in Zion, to give them beauty for ashes, the oil of joy for mourning, the garment of praise for the spirit of heaviness; That they may be called trees of righteousness, the planting of the Lord, that He may be glorified. And they shall rebuild the old ruins, they shall raise up the former desolations, and they shall repair the ruined cities, the desolations of many generations."

God never leaves ruins unattended. He rebuilds what others abandon. Your healing is not just for you; it's generational. When you rise, others find the courage to rebuild, too.

Beauty for ashes is not a metaphor; it's a promise. Redemption means your mourning will not have the final word. God replaces the heaviness of your past with the praise of your present.

The fragments of your life are becoming foundations of faith for others.

JOURNAL *Reflection* 

☑ What "ashes" in your life is God turning into beauty?

....

....

....

....

....

☑ What parts of your story can now serve as "rebuilding stones" for someone else?

....

....

....

....

....

PRAYER OF *Healing and Encouragement*

Father,

Thank You for being the God who rebuilds what life has shattered. Thank you for seeing value in the fragments others have overlooked. Today, I offer You every piece of me, the broken, the mended, and the hidden, and I trust You to make it whole.

Redeem my memories, Lord. Let every scar sing of Your faithfulness. Turn my mourning into dancing, my loss into learning, and my pain into purpose.

I declare that nothing in my life is wasted. Every moment is being rewritten by grace. And I will tell my story, not from my wounds, but from my healing. In Jesus' name, Amen.

PERSONAL *Reflection*

CHAPTER

Six

WHEN ATTACHMENTS SHAPE YOUR SOUL

Chapter Overview

Wholeness doesn't end with honesty; it deepens when we confront the bonds that quietly control our hearts. This chapter reveals how unhealed trauma can form emotional attachments that feel like love but lead to bondage. These "soul ties" can keep us clinging to what drains us, repeating patterns that feel familiar but never free.

The author reminds us that healing means learning to release the counterfeit connections, those relationships, memories, or behaviors rooted in brokenness rather than peace. Through faith, reflection, and renewed boundaries, you can break cycles of pain and step into relationships that reflect God's design for love, safety, and purpose.

Expanded Insight

From both a spiritual and psychological perspective, unhealthy attachments distort identity. When love and pain coexist, the heart learns confusion instead of comfort. These trauma bonds feel deep but are deceptive; they are connections born from shared wounds instead of shared wholeness. As a Licensed Professional Counselor, Ellasin explains that trauma bonds often mirror early experiences of conditional love, neglect, or rejection. They thrive on cycles of affection and withdrawal, moments of validation followed by emotional distance. This pattern, known as intermittent reinforcement, creates dependency. Spiritually, it becomes bondage masquerading as intimacy.

True love brings freedom; counterfeit love brings captivity. Healing begins when we allow God to prune what no longer serves our growth.

REFLECTIVE *Questions*

☑ What relationships or attachments in your life have left you feeling more drained than strengthened?

....

....

....

....

☑ How have patterns from past trauma influenced the way you give and receive love?

....

....

....

....

☑ What does freedom in relationships look like for you today?

....

....

....

☑ In what ways has God revealed that certain "connections" were really distractions from your healing?

55

....

....

....

....

☑ How can you begin replacing false attachments with a deeper attachment to God's Word and presence?

....

....

....

....

INTERACTIVE *Activities* 

1. Attachment Inventory

Create two columns in your journal: "Connections That Heal" and "Connections That Drain." List the people, habits, or memories that belong in each. Pray over the second list, asking God to help you release what does not serve His purpose for your life (see 2 Corinthians 6:14).

2. Breaking the Cycle Reflection

Write about a time when you mistook chaos for connection. What did you learn about yourself and your needs? How has God been teaching you to redefine love through His truth?

3. Healthy Bond Declarations

Speak these aloud daily:

"I am no longer bound by counterfeit connections."

"I am worthy of safe, healthy love."

"My peace is protected by God's presence."

Add your own affirmation about freedom and identity in Christ.

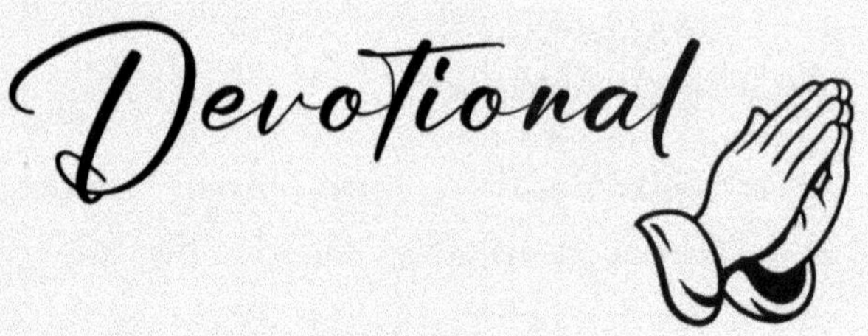

PSALM 147:3 (NKJV),

"He heals the brokenhearted and binds up their wounds."

JOHN 8:36,

"Therefore if the Son makes you free, you shall be free indeed."

ROMANS 12:2,

"And do not be conformed to this world, but be transformed by the renewing of your mind, that you may prove what is that good and acceptable and perfect will of God."

When attachments are shaped by pain, they imprison the soul. But when love is rooted in Christ, it liberates. Healing begins when we let God redefine love for us. The same God who binds wounds also unties unhealthy bonds. Freedom is not found in forgetting; it's found in surrendering.

Every time you release a toxic tie, Heaven celebrates a new level of your healing. You are not losing people, you are gaining peace.

JOURNAL *Reflection*

☑ What emotional or relational ties might God be asking you to release?

....

....

....

....

☑ What new, life-giving attachments is He inviting you to embrace?

....

....

....

....

☑ How does your relationship with God model the kind of connection you now desire with others?

....

....

....

PRAYER OF *Release* and *Renewal*

Father,

Thank you for revealing the places where my soul has been tied to pain. Today, I choose to release every attachment that keeps me from Your peace. Cut the cords that connect me to confusion, manipulation, and fear. Heal the parts of me that accepted chaos as love.

Teach me to recognize authentic connection, the kind rooted in truth, safety, and grace. Surround me with relationships that nourish my purpose and reflect Your heart. Renew my mind so that I may love without losing myself and give without compromising my worth.

I declare that I am free, whole, and deeply loved. My identity is secure in You.

In Jesus' name, Amen.

PERSONAL *Reflection*

CHAPTER
Seven
THE COST OF BELONGING

Chapter Overview

Belonging is a beautiful desire, but when we've been wounded, it can come with a price. Many of us have paid for belonging with pieces of ourselves: compromising identity, silencing truth, or shrinking to fit the spaces that couldn't contain our light.

This chapter invites you to explore where you've overpaid for acceptance and undervalued your worth. True belonging doesn't demand your brokenness; it welcomes your wholeness. You were never meant to beg for inclusion when God has already seated you in His presence.

Expanded Insight

From a psychological perspective, the human need to belong is deeply rooted; we are wired for connection. Yet trauma can distort that need, leading us to seek belonging through unhealthy attachments, performance, or people-pleasing.

CHAPTER SEVEN

Spiritually, this is the struggle between being approved by people and being accepted by God. When belonging comes at the cost of peace, authenticity, or purpose, it becomes bondage.

Jesus experienced rejection but never compromised His identity for connection. He didn't belong everywhere, and neither will you. That's not rejection; it's redirection.

You were created for covenant, not convenience. When you stop trying to earn belonging, you make space for God to bring relationships that match your healed identity.

REFLECTIVE *Questions*

- ☑ Where in your life have you compromised your truth to be accepted?

....

....

....

....

- ☑ What internal message do you hear when you feel left out or overlooked?

....

....

....

....

- ☑ How does God's acceptance of you redefine what belonging looks like?

....

....

....

☑ What relationships or spaces have become too costly to your peace?

....

....

....

....

☑ How can you begin building connections rooted in authenticity rather than approval?

....

....

....

....

☑ What boundaries do you need to put in place to protect your sense of belonging in Christ?

....

....

....

....

INTERACTIVE *Activities* 

1. The Circle Exercise

Draw three circles on a page: Inner Circle, Middle Circle, Outer Circle. List people in each based on their closeness and impact. Ask yourself:

- Who belongs in my inner circle?
- Who have I allowed too close without discernment?
- Who needs to be loved from a healthy distance?

2. The Belonging Statement

Write a declaration that begins with:

"I belong because God says I do. I no longer seek permission to exist in spaces that reject who I am becoming."

Read this daily until it settles into your heart.

3. Soul Audit

Reflect on your environments, work, church, friendships, and family. Ask: "Do I feel free here, or do I feel like I must perform?" Commit to honoring the spaces where you can be your authentic self.

Devotional

GALATIANS 1:10 (NKJV)

"For do I now persuade men, or God? Or do I seek to please men? For if I still pleased men, I would not be a bondservant of Christ."

Paul's words remind us that pleasing people and serving Christ often stand in tension. Belonging to God requires releasing the need to be validated by others. When you live from a place of divine acceptance, human rejection no longer defines you.

Jesus knew the cost of belonging. He was rejected, so you could be received. Your healing begins when you stop auditioning for approval and start resting in identity.

JOURNAL *Reflection*

☑ What relationships does God want to reorder in your life?

....

....

....

....

....

☑ How does belonging to Christ reshape your sense of self-worth?

....

....

....

....

....

PRAYER OF *Healing and Encouragement*

Father,

Thank you for calling me yours. Thank You for seeing me when others overlooked me, for welcoming me when I felt unworthy to belong. Forgive me for the times I've traded my peace for approval or hidden my truth to fit in.

Teach me to discern which spaces are safe and which are suffocating. Help me to embrace belongings that don't cost my soul. May I find rest in the truth that I am already accepted, loved, and chosen by You.

Let every false connection fall away, and every divine relationship be restored. I belong to You, and that is enough.

In Jesus' name, Amen.

PERSONAL *Reflection*

CHAPTER

Eight

WHEN THE SOUL REMEMBERS

Chapter Overview

The soul never forgets what the mind tries to suppress. Even after years of moving forward, a sound, scent, or moment can awaken memories buried deep within. This chapter invites you to understand what happens when the soul remembers, not to reopen wounds, but to release what still lingers.

Healing does not erase memory; it transforms how memory affects you. When the soul remembers, God reminds you that every recall is not for pain, but for processing. He wants to redeem what your heart still holds and bring peace to what your body still carries.

Expanded Insight

In the field of trauma therapy, it's often said: "The body keeps the score and the soul keeps receipts." Emotional experiences, especially those tied to trauma, are stored not just in the brain but in the body and soul. When these memories resurface, it's not regression, it's revelation.

Spiritually, these memories are opportunities for deeper healing. They come not to torment you, but to show you what still needs God's touch. Unprocessed memories can trigger emotional reactions that feel disproportionate to the present moment. But through prayer, awareness, and truth, you can learn to respond instead of reacting.

When your soul remembers, don't run, reflect. God is not exposing you to shame you; He's revealing the root so He can restore the fruit.

REFLECTIVE *Questions*

☑ What memories or triggers still stir deep emotion within you?

....

....

....

....

☑ How do these moments impact your relationships or sense of safety?

....

....

....

....

☑ When you feel emotionally triggered, how can you pause and invite God into that moment?

....

....

....

☑ What would it look like to trust God with the memories that still hurt?

....

....

....

....

☑ How can remembering become a step toward releasing?

....

....

....

....

☑ What truth from God's Word can replace a painful memory you've been holding onto?

....

....

....

....

INTERACTIVE *Activities* 

1. **Memory Mapping Exercise**

    On a blank sheet, write the earliest memory that still brings you emotional discomfort. Beneath it, write how it shaped your view of yourself or others. Next, write what God's truth says about that situation. Example: "They abandoned me" → "God will never leave me nor forsake me" (Hebrews 13:5).

2. **The Soul Release Prayer Practice**

    When an old memory surfaces, say aloud:

    "God, I acknowledge this memory. I release its power over me. Heal the parts of me that still remember pain instead of peace."

3. **Music and Memory Healing**

    Create a worship playlist that comforts your spirit. Each time your soul remembers, let praise replace the pain. Worship invites peace where memory once held fear.

PSALM 34:18–19 (NKJV)

"The Lord is near to those who have a broken heart and saves such as have a contrite spirit. Many are the afflictions of the righteous, but the Lord delivers him out of them all."

When the soul remembers, God draws near. He doesn't shame you for what surfaces. He shelters you in His presence. David's psalm reminds us that brokenness is not a flaw; it's an invitation for divine nearness.

Every remembered pain is a place where God desires to dwell. Every tear is evidence that you survived what once threatened to destroy you. The Lord delivers, not once, but continually.

Let His nearness bring new meaning to what your soul recalls.

JOURNAL *Reflection*

☑ What moment from your past do you sense God revisiting with compassion?

....

....

....

....

....

☑ How does knowing God is near comfort you when old pain resurfaces?

....

....

....

....

....

PRAYER OF *Healing and Encouragement*

Father,

When my soul remembers, let me remember you first. You were there in every moment, even when I couldn't see You. You are the God who heals what memory cannot erase.

I release every recollection still wrapped in pain. Redeem my memories, Lord. Let them no longer hold me hostage but lead me to healing. When the past whispers fear, let Your truth speak louder.

Teach my soul to rest in peace, not replay pain. And when memories arise, remind me that they're not signs of brokenness, they're reminders of Your faithfulness.

In Jesus' name, Amen.

PERSONAL *Reflection*

CHAPTER
Nine
WHEN LOVE HURTS

Chapter Overview

Love is meant to heal, but sometimes it hurts. This chapter explores what happens when love, the very thing that should nurture us, becomes the source of our deepest wounds. Whether through betrayal, abandonment, manipulation, or unmet expectations, painful love can shape how we see God, ourselves, and others.

But this is not a story of defeat, it's one of discovery. God wants to heal the distorted image of love that pain created. The love that wounded you is not the same love that will heal you.

As you walk through this chapter, you will learn to separate love's pain from love's truth, to understand that God's love is not what broke you, but what is restoring you.

Expanded Insight

In psychology, attachment wounds, often called relational trauma, occur when the people we depend on for safety become the source of our hurt. These experiences can create internal confusion: "How can something that felt like love also hurt me so deeply?"

Spiritually, God uses even these moments to reveal what love truly is. Love without truth becomes manipulation; love without boundaries becomes a form of bondage. True love heals because it reflects the nature of God, patient, kind, steadfast, and freeing (1 Corinthians 13:4-7).

When love hurts, God steps in to redefine what love means through His Word. He reminds you that His love is not possessive, conditional, or controlling. His love corrects without condemning, comforts without crippling, and restores without requiring you to lose yourself.

Your pain does not make you unworthy of love; it makes you aware of your need for divine love.

REFLECTIVE *Questions*

☑ When you think about love, what emotions surface first: peace, fear, disappointment, or hope?

....

....

....

....

☑ How has the past hurt influenced the way you receive love from others or from God?

....

....

....

....

☑ In what ways have you confused pain with passion or control with care?

....

....

....

☑ How do you define love now, after your healing journey has begun?

....

....

....

....

☑ What would it look like to love from a healed place rather than a hurting one?

....

....

....

....

☑ Who in your life needs to experience love expressed through your growth and boundaries?

....

....

....

....

INTERACTIVE *Activities* 

1. **Redefining Love Exercise**

   Write down the ways love has hurt you, emotionally, mentally, or spiritually. Next to each, write what healthy love should have looked like. Example: "They controlled me" → "Love respects freedom." This helps retrain your mind to recognize healthy versus harmful love.

2. **Boundaries of the Heart Map**

   Draw a heart in the center of your page. Around it, write boundaries that protect your peace: honesty, communication, respect, and prayer. Inside the heart, write what you'll allow to stay: forgiveness, compassion, patience.

3. **Letter of Release**

   Write a letter to the person, relationship, or version of yourself that experienced love's pain. Say: "I release you. I forgive. I choose peace." Tear or safely burn the paper as a symbolic act of letting go.

Devotional

ROMANS 8:38–39 (NKJV)

"For I am persuaded that neither death nor life, nor angels nor principalities nor powers, nor things present nor things to come, nor height nor depth, nor any other created thing, shall be able to separate us from the love of God which is in Christ Jesus our Lord."

There is no wound deep enough to separate you from the love of God. Human love may have failed you, but divine love remains constant. God's love is not fragile; it's fierce, faithful, and forever.

Paul's words remind us that love is not measured by perfection, but by presence. Even when love hurts, God's love heals. He doesn't withdraw when you're broken; He draws closer.

Let His love rewrite the definition of what love should feel like.

JOURNAL *Reflection*

✓ How has God's love redefined your understanding of what love truly is?

....

....

....

....

....

✓ What part of your heart still struggles to trust love again?

....

....

....

....

....

PRAYER OF *Healing* and *Encouragement*

Father,

You are love, and in You, there is no fear. I confess that love has hurt me, confused me, and even made me question my worth. But today, I choose to believe that Your love is greater than my pain.

Heal my heart where love went wrong. Restore my capacity to trust without losing discernment, and to give without losing myself. Teach me to love from a whole place, to love wisely, freely, and purely.

Thank You for showing me that love is not manipulation or control, but freedom and grace. Let my heart reflect Your kind of love, patient, steadfast, and true.

In Jesus' name, Amen.

PERSONAL *Reflection*

CHAPTER *Ten*

BREAKING THE SILENCE

Chapter Overview

There comes a moment in every healing journey when silence becomes too heavy to carry. For years, many of us have kept secrets, not because we wanted to, but because pain taught us that our voices didn't matter. Fear, shame, and rejection convinced us to hide what needed to be heard.

This chapter is about reclaiming your voice. Breaking the silence is not about exposing others; it's about freeing yourself. It's about releasing the sound of truth that has been trapped inside your soul.

When you speak your story, you shift from surviving to healing. Your silence may have protected you once, but now your voice will empower you and others to live free.

Expanded Insight

Silence can be both a survival mechanism and a prison. Psychologically, many trauma survivors remain silent out of fear, fear of disbelief, retaliation, or rejection. Yet silence also reinforces shame, convincing us that our truth is too much to handle.

Spiritually, God invites you to break the silence not in anger, but in authority. Proverbs 31:8 says, "Speak up for those who cannot speak for themselves." When you speak, you not only free yourself, you open the door for others still bound by secrecy and pain.

Jesus modeled this courage when He confronted injustice and spoke truth, even when it cost Him. He shows us that healing requires voice, not vengeance.

Breaking the silence is sacred; it's the sound of chains falling.

REFLECTIVE *Questions*

☑ What truths have you been afraid to speak out loud?

....

....

....

....

☑ What emotions rise when you think about breaking your silence?

....

....

....

....

☑ How has silence protected you, and how has it also held you back?

....

....

....

....

☑ What would it look like to use your voice with both wisdom and grace?

....

....

....

....

☑ Who in your life represents a safe space to share your truth?

....

....

....

....

☑ How can your testimony become a source of healing for others?

....

....

....

....

INTERACTIVE *Activities* 

1. **"Voice Unlocked" Exercise**

    Find a quiet place. Take a deep breath and say aloud:

    "My voice matters. My truth is safe with God. I no longer carry the weight of silence." Repeat until your spirit begins to agree with your words.

2. **The Safe Person List**

    Write down 3–5 people who make you feel emotionally safe, individuals who listen without judgment and handle truth with care. Ask God for discernment about who can hold your story with wisdom.

3. **Testimony Timeline**

    Create a simple timeline of key events that shaped your story, both painful and redemptive moments. Beside each event, write how you see God's hand, even in the silence. Use this as a guide for sharing your story when the time is right.

Devotional

PSALM 32:3–5 (NKJV)

"When I kept silent, my bones grew old through my groaning all the day long. For day and night, Your hand was heavy upon me; My vitality was turned into the drought of summer. I acknowledged my sin to You, and my iniquity I have not hidden. I said, 'I will confess my transgressions to the Lord,' And You forgave the iniquity of my sin."

David describes the weight of silence, the exhaustion that comes from carrying truth unspoken. But when he finally confessed and released what was hidden, forgiveness and freedom followed.

In the same way, unspoken pain drains the soul. When you break the silence, whether through confession, counseling, prayer, or journaling, healing begins to flow again.

God is not waiting to punish you for speaking; He's waiting to heal you through it.

JOURNAL *Reflection*

☑ What area of your life has grown weary from silence?

....

....

....

....

....

☑ What freedom might await you on the other side of honesty?

....

....

....

....

....

PRAYER OF *Healing and Encouragement*

Father,

You are the God who hears even the cries I never spoke. Thank you for reminding me that my silence does not define my strength; my honesty does.

Give me the courage to use my voice for healing, not harm. Teach me when to speak and when to stay silent, but never let fear be my reason for silence again.

Break every chain that has bound my words. Let my voice carry truth, hope, and freedom for myself and others. I declare that my story belongs to You, and it will glorify Your name.

In Jesus' name, Amen.

PERSONAL *Reflection*

CHAPTER
Eleven
RECLAIMING MY POWER

Chapter Overview

Reclaiming your power isn't about control; it's about choice. For too long, pain, fear, and people may have dictated how you saw yourself and what you believed you deserved. But healing restores your ability to choose differently.

This chapter invites you to take back your emotional, spiritual, and mental authority. You are not powerless. You are not defined by what happened to you, but by what you decide to do next with God's strength.

When you reclaim your power, you are not taking it from others; you are reclaiming what God gave you: self-worth, confidence, peace, and purpose.

Expanded Insight

In trauma recovery, one of the most transformative stages is empowerment. After seasons of surviving, your body and soul begin to realize: "I have choices now." This shift, from helplessness to agency, is sacred.

Spiritually, God calls you to walk in that same empowerment. Luke 10:19 reminds us, "Behold, I give you the authority to trample on serpents and scorpions, and over all the power of the enemy." Healing is not passive. It's active participation with the Spirit of God to reclaim dominion over your mind, emotions, and future.

You reclaim power every time you say no to what once drained you, yes to what aligns with peace, and amen to God's purpose for your life.

REFLECTIVE *Questions*

- ☑ Where in your life have you given away your power, emotionally, mentally, or spiritually?

....

....

....

....

- ☑ What does personal empowerment mean to you as a believer?

....

....

....

....

- ☑ What boundaries need to be rebuilt to protect your peace?

....

....

....

☑ How can you walk in authority without becoming defensive or controlling?

....

....

....

....

☑ What small decision today would represent you reclaiming your power?

....

....

....

....

☑ How does God's Word affirm your strength and authority in Him?

....

....

....

....

INTERACTIVE *Activities* 

1. Power Reclaiming Declaration

Stand in front of a mirror and say aloud:

"I reclaim my power through Christ. I release fear. I release shame. I choose to stand in truth, peace, and strength. I am not powerless, I am redeemed."

Repeat daily until your spirit begins to respond with confidence instead of fear.

2. Boundary Rebuilding Chart

Draw three columns labeled: People, Places, and Practices. List what drains you under each. Then beside it, write new boundaries that honor your peace (e.g., "Limit time spent," "Communicate needs clearly," "Pray before saying yes").

3. My Power Prayer Journal

Write a short daily prayer asking God to show you one area where you can reclaim your voice, your time, or your peace. Reflect each week on how those choices are reshaping your confidence.

2 TIMOTHY 1:7 (NKJV)

"For God has not given us a spirit of fear, but of power and of love and of a sound mind."

Fear is not your inheritance; power is. God didn't call you to walk timidly through life; He called you to walk in authority through His Spirit.

To reclaim your power is to remember who you are in Him. It's the moment you stop apologizing for existing and start standing on the Word that declares you are chosen, equipped, and empowered.

You have the right to peace. You have the authority to change your story. Your strength is not rebellion, it's restoration.

JOURNAL *Reflection* 

☑ What fears have limited your confidence or kept you silent?

....

....

....

....

....

☑ What does it look like for you to walk daily in God-given power?

....

....

....

....

....

PRAYER OF *Healing and Encouragement*

Father,

Thank you for reminding me that I am not powerless. You have given me authority over fear, peace over panic, and purpose over pain.

Today, I reclaim the power You placed within me, the power to forgive, to choose peace, and to walk boldly in who You've called me to be. I broke the agreement with every lie that said I wasn't enough.

Empower me to live from truth, not trauma. Let every decision I make flow from confidence in Your Word. Help me to stand in my identity, bold, healed, and free.

In Jesus' name, Amen.

PERSONAL *Reflection*

CHAPTER

Twelve

BECOMING WHOLE

Chapter Overview

Wholeness is not perfection; it's peace. It's living in harmony with who God created you to be: spirit, soul, and body united under His love. Becoming whole doesn't mean life is free of pain; it means pain no longer controls the narrative.

This chapter reminds you that healing was never about returning to who you were; it's about stepping into who you're becoming. Wholeness is the evidence of a healed soul, when what once shattered you becomes what strengthens you.

God doesn't just restore what was lost; He restores what was meant to be.

Expanded Insight

Psychologically, wholeness involves integration, the uniting of every part of the self that was once fragmented by trauma, shame, or fear. Spiritually, it's the process of aligning your identity with God's truth rather than your past experiences.

To become whole is to live without inner division, to let your mind, emotions, and spirit work together rather than against each other. It's when your "yes" means yes, your "no" means no, and your peace becomes your compass.

Jesus asked the man at the pool of Bethesda, "Do you want to be made whole?" (John 5:6). That question still echoes today. Wholeness is a choice, an agreement to live healed, not just helped.

When you choose wholeness, you choose freedom over familiarity.

REFLECTIVE *Questions*

✓ What does wholeness mean to you personally?

....

....

....

....

✓ How does being whole differ from being healed?

....

....

....

....

✓ What areas of your life still need alignment with God's peace?

....

....

....

....

☑ How can you daily nurture the spiritual, emotional, and physical parts of yourself?

....

....

....

....

☑ What evidence of wholeness can you already see in your life?

....

....

....

....

☑ How can your wholeness become a ministry to others?

....

....

....

....

INTERACTIVE *Activities* 

1. **"Whole Self" Reflection Wheel**

Draw a circle divided into three sections: Spirit, Soul, and Body. Write what each part needs to thrive (e.g., prayer, rest, community, healthy food, joy). Ask yourself: "Am I nurturing each area equally?"

2. **Morning Wholeness Affirmation**

Each morning, speak this aloud:

"Today I choose Wholeness. I am not fragmented. I am aligned with peace, anchored in faith, and filled with God's love." Repeat it until your heart believes it.

3. **Gratitude Healing Practice**

Write down three things each day that reflect your growth, not what's perfect, but what's progressing. Wholeness grows through gratitude.

Devotional

1 THESSALONIANS 5:23 (NKJV)

"Now may the God of peace Himself sanctify you completely; and may your whole spirit, soul, and body be preserved blameless at the coming of our Lord Jesus Christ."

Paul's prayer reveals that God is not just interested in saving your soul; He wants to make every part of you whole. Wholeness is divine alignment, when peace reigns in your heart, mind, and body.

You were never meant to live fragmented. The God of peace desires to make you complete, not lacking in any good thing. As you surrender daily, wholeness becomes your lifestyle, not just your goal.

You are becoming who you were always meant to be, whole, healed, and free.

JOURNAL *Reflection*

☑ What does it look like for God to "sanctify you completely"?

....

....

....

....

....

☑ How will you preserve your peace and protect your wholeness going forward?

....

....

....

....

....

PRAYER OF *Healing and Encouragement*

Father,

Thank You for leading me through every chapter of healing and bringing me to the place of wholeness. You have touched every part of me, mind, body, and spirit, and reminded me that I am not broken beyond repair.

Help me to walk daily in alignment with Your peace. Let wholeness become my new normal. May every step I take reflect the freedom, wisdom, and grace I've gained through this journey.

Thank You that I am not who I was, I am who You've called me to be. Whole. Loved. Free.

In Jesus' name, Amen.

PERSONAL *Reflection*

MY FINAL

Declaration

I AM THE HEALED SOUL

Even with all of that, I can say now that my journey was worth it. Every broken relationship, every tear-stained pillow, sleepless night, every misstep led me to the arms of a God who never let me go. I am a living witness that He restores what is shattered and redeems what is lost. I am not just surviving; I am a testimony of His goodness and grace.

I went from broken to golden. It reminds me of Kintsugi, the traditional Japanese art of repairing fractured ceramics by mending the pieces with a lacquer mixed with powdered gold, silver, or platinum. This technique, also known as Kintsukuroi ('golden repair'), treats breakage and repair as part of an object's history, rather than something to conceal. It creates a more beautiful and stronger piece by highlighting the golden seams.

Acknowledgments

I give glory to God for His faithfulness, wisdom, and healing power. Thank You, Lord, for entrusting me with this assignment to bring hope and healing to others.

To my husband, Pastor Eric Allen, thank you for your love, strength, and unwavering support. To my family, friends, and church community, thank you for your prayers and encouragement.

To every reader walking this journey, thank you for trusting me with your story. Remember, healing is not a one-time event; it's a daily walk with God.

NOTES 

NOTES 

Notes 

NOTES 

NOTES 

NOTES 

NOTES 

Notes 

Notes 

NOTES